UNDERSTANDING
ISLAM
The Mystery Religion

UNDERSTANDING ISLAM
by ED DECKER
ISBN# 1-60039-180-X

Pubished by LAMP POST INC.
www.lamppostpubs.com

A Publication of
Saints Alive In Jesus
P.O. Box 1347
Issaquah, WA 98027
USA
ed@SaintsAlive.com
www.SaintsAlive.com

Cover design by
Michelle De Monnin for
De Monnin's Art Studio

Unless otherwise indicated,
all Scripture quotations are
taken from The King James
Version of the Bible.

Copyright © 2002, 2010 by
J. Edward Decker
Saints Alive In Jesus

Portions of this report are taken from the Chapter on Islam in Ed Decker's book, **FAST FACTS ON FALSE TEACHINGS**, co-authored with Dr. Ron Carlson, published by Harvest House Publishers, Eugene, OR. You can order copies of the complete book at www.saintsalive.com at your Christian bookstore.

Printed in the United States of America. All rights reserved under International Copyright Law. Contents and/or cover (whether in printed or ebook format, or any other published derivation) may not be reproduced in whole or in part in any form without the express written consent of the Publisher. Unauthorized duplication is a violation of applicable laws.

UNDERSTANDING ISLAM

The Mystery Religion

by ED DECKER

DEDICATION

I dedicate this booklet to the many men and women of the armed services who have stepped forward to lay their lives on the line to bring freedom to those held in the bondage of Islamic fundamentalism. I believe they are opening the door for the good news of Jesus Christ to be brought to hundreds of millions of Muslims who have never heard the gospel.

INTRODUCTION

LIKE THE REST OF THE COUNTRY, I was shocked and stunned by the violence and terror of September 11, 2001. Carol and I were at a pastors' retreat and were awakened with a call to turn on our TV. What we saw was almost surreal, an incomprehensible sight. We wept as we watched. Rushing into our clothes, we hurried and joined the other pastors in the conference room where we went into a time of fervent prayer and intercession. As the events unfolded, I knew that, as a nation, we would be facing the most serious attack in the history of our country. I also knew it would come through the ranks of a religion, not another nation.

A few years ago, I read a book called "The Islamic Invasion," by Dr. Robert Morey, (1992 edition Harvest House Publishers). Dr. Morey said, "the very DNA of every fervent Muslim, through persuasion and through the sword, is to take the world for Allah. It has been a holy calling from the time of Mohammed's journey to Medina, where he built an army over 10,000 zealots and proclaimed Allah had instructed them to go forth and cause the nations to bow to Allah and recognize him as Allah's holy prophet or suffer the sword as infidels *(ed: non-Muslims)*".

Throughout the centuries, the flames of that fire burned across the nations, whole cities converting or being slaughtered. That holy war still rages across the world and non-Muslims continue to be slain in vast, incomprehensible numbers. Dr. Morey's book was a prophetic wake up call to America. Not only would that battlefield come to America, but it would hit us with a new level of violence never seen before on this land.

THE BATTLE IS HERE

IT IS ISLAMIC IDEOLOGY THAT THE world is divided into two: The Islamic "Dar e-Salaam" or House of Islam or House of Peace. Opposing this "Dar e-Salaam" is the "Dar e-Harb" or

House of War into which all infidels fall. There can be no peace for Islam until the entire "Dar e-Harb" falls to the "Dar e-Salaam". So this is a fight to the finish. Islam must be victorious or be vanquished. There can be no effective defense against Islam or any effective Christian outreach to its people until we understand this volatile religious challenger of our faith and our way of life.

We must understand that the large majority of Muslims living in the United Sates have come here to live lives of peace and prosperity. Many have said that life here is wonderful, marvelous. They contribute much to our society. Many fathers and husbands are able to release their daughters and wives to live life freely, openly, without degradation or sexual mutilation in the name of Allah. They can go to school, be educated, have careers, drive cars, go to the movies and marry whom they love.

After speaking to many who study these things, I would guess that over 90% of the Muslims in America live such lives in peace, having Americanized their faith without compromising their beliefs.

IT'S JUST A TENTH OF A TENTH OF A TENTH
However, that leaves 10% who maintain the fundamentalism of radical Islam. The percentage is small, but the actual number of such Muslims in America alone is about 600,000.

If we took just ten percent of that number, we would have 60,000 Muslims here who maintain that America is the great Satan the Islamic extremists shout about. In their minds, we must either bow to Allah or be slain in his holy name. A tenth of that small minority leaves us with a pool of about 6,000 extremist Muslims with the potential for terrorist behavior. These are such as those who attacked us on September 11, 2001, living here among us, as an Islamic Fifth Column. For those too young to remember the Second World War, a Fifth Column is a group of people, although residing, even as citizens of the United States, act traitorously and subversively on behalf of an enemy.

On a global basis, with over a billion Muslims and dealing with just 20% falling into this fundamentalist group, we have 200 million fundamentalists and over 20 million Muslims who have a Jihad world view. Following my one tenth of one percent formula, we are left with a pool of over 2 million fanatic zealots out there who can easily become "terrorists for Allah." (ed: Jahid: 1: a holy war waged on behalf of Islam as a religious duty 2: a crusade for a principle or belief , Merriam Webster Collegiate Dictionary)

My estimates in this area were confirmed when I recently watched an MSNBC special report during which an expert calculated that she (a Dr. Hunter) estimated the number of extreme radicals in countries where Islam is in the majority, to be double my figures.

This is going to be a long and difficult war against the likes of Osama bin Laden and we must know what we are dealing with. Through all this, we must never let fear and anger against that one tenth of one percent jade our hearts and actions against those who live among us as friends and neighbors. We must let them see the love of Christ in us, remembering that we are all made in His image, and His Son died for us all. Anything less would be to deny the call of Christ in our lives.

President Bush commented recently that while we need to be in a state of high alert and we should not fall into a state of fear or revenge. As Christians, we need to be in intercession for this people group and prepare ourselves to be His hand extended. We must be His ambassadors, girded up and prepared according to Chapter 6th of the book of Ephesians, with our feet shod with the preparation of the gospel of peace so we may open our mouths boldly to make known the mystery of the gospel.

ACCIDENTALLY STIRRING THE WRATH OF ISLAM

A few years ago, I was speaking at Utah State University in Logan, Utah on the subject, **"Mormonism — the American Islam."** I drew a comparison between the amazingly similar claims of Mohammed and Joseph Smith. Both men claimed visitations of an angel of light, the claim as God's last and greatest prophet, and the claim that they were called to bring forth God's final Word for mankind: the Koran and the Book of Mormon.

I compared their similar doctrines of the nature of God, personal salvation and the after life with those of orthodox Christianity. The auditorium became too small for the large gathering, and we filled the large commons area of the Student Union beyond capacity. We finally overflowed throughout the large student center and entrance.

USU had certainly grown from that small Agricultural College I attended in the early 1950s. The meeting was packed with Muslims and Islamic clerics, extremely offended at any reference to Allah, the Koran and very angry that I would draw as offensive a comparison as any similarity to Mormonism.

During the presentation of my evidence, there was much murmuring and shouting. When I opened the floor for the "Question and Answer" time, I faced a number of very agitated and verbally abusive Muslims. In fact, the Muslim interaction completely overshadowed any dialogue on Mormonism. Were there not security guards all around, I am sure there would have been serious difficulties. The next day, I met with two local Muslim leaders and began a series of dialogues that forced me to take a deep look at Islam's history, tenets of belief and its comparisons to orthodox Christianity.

Today, the more than 6 million Muslims in the United States add up to more than all the Mormons, Jehovah's Witnesses and Christian Scientists combined. An extremely militant proselytizing program is under way in many major cities and in every State University we have visited. The

Muslims may soon make the Mormon missionary effort look pale in comparison. As orthodox Christians, we are going to have to be ready to deal with what may be the most aggressive assault on Christianity in its history.

THE FAITH OF MOHAMMED

Let's look at the faith of Mohammed. When he was born in Mecca in 570 AD, the black Kaaba was the religious center of all Arabia. In Mohammed's day, approximately 360 idols were worshipped there, standing in the great courtyard. One of those deities or *Allahs* was the god of the Quarish tribe, of which Mohammed was a member. When the Quarish tribe took control of Mecca, all the idols except Allah, the idol of their tribe, were destroyed.

The Koran tells us that Mohammed drove the other idols away; his god was now the only god and he was its messenger. But he kept the Kaaba as a holy, sacred place. He obligated every believer to make a pilgrimage to the stone at least once in his lifetime. (Sura 22:26-37)

The central prayer or declaration of Islam, to this day, is: *"There is no God but (this) Allah and Mohammed is his prophet."*

Many people believe that Islam, Judaism and Christianity are all just kissing cousins. In fact, many Christians erroneously teach that Allah is just another name for the Biblical God whom we worship. Hopefully, this comes from ignorance rather than ecumenical foolishness.

In this study, I am going to examine Islam from the orthodox Christian perspective, what it is that Muslims teach and believe, and how it differs from Christianity. Let's equip you to share the claims of Jesus Christ in a loving and compassionate way with the Muslim.

A WORD TO THE MUSLIM READER

Muslims will be reading these words as well as Christians and I want to address those readers for just a moment. Muslims need to know that I appreciate you taking the time to see how your faith stands from the Christian viewpoint. There may be some things that you read with which you will be in strong disagreement. I apologize for offending you, but I will speak out on the issue. I know of no other way in which we can dialogue honestly.

We need to dialogue these issues in truth and in love for one another. *As the Book of Proverbs says: As iron sharpens iron, So a man sharpens the countenance of his friend.* (Prov. 27:17 NKJV) We need to stand on words of truth that will bring us all to God's perspective in this matter.

> *All the paths of the LORD are mercy and truth,*
> *To such as keep His covenant and His testimonies.*
> *(Psalms 25:10)*
>
> *Oh, send out Your light and Your truth!*
> *Let them lead me... (Psalms 43:3)*
>
> *Sanctify them by Your truth.*
> *Your word is truth. (John 17:17)*
>
> And mix not truth with falsehood, nor conceal the truth (i.e. Muhammad Peace be upon him is Alláh's Messenger and his qualities are written in your Scriptures, the Taurát (Torah) and the Injeel (Gospel)) while you know (the truth). (Sura 2:42)

Please understand that in a western country where the freedom of religion and freedom of speech are constitutional guarantees, we have the freedom to discuss, to consider and to think, concerning religious issues. We are not in countries such as Saudi Arabia, or Iran where we would have religious police at our doors, confiscating such studies as this, because in such nations there simply is no freedom of religion. There is no freedom of thought and action. You cannot question Mohammed or the Koran.

But we are not in a Muslim nation. We are in a Christian nation where our democratic constitution gives us the freedom to think and act for ourselves. In things of faith, this is so vitally important and as such, is a major difference between our cultures and faiths. The value of dialogue brings greater appreciation and meaning to things of faith.

ISLAM ACROSS THE WORLD

Islam is a rapidly growing religion, both spiritually and geographically. Today, Islam makes up about one-sixth of the world's population. At this writing, in late 2001, there are approximately one billion, three hundred million (1.3 billion) Muslims in the world. Islam now dominates both the religious and political processes in almost 60 countries of the world.

Surprisingly, when most people think about Muslims, they immediately think of the Middle East or North Africa, but in fact, only twenty per cent (20%) of the world's Muslims live in the Middle East or North Africa. Most of them live in other countries.

The Arab world all together, including all of the Middle East and North Africa, has under two hundred (200) million Muslims. The largest Muslim country is Indonesia, with one hundred and eighty-two (182) million Muslims, 80% of its population. Bangladesh has one hundred and Fifteen (115) million, 88% of its population. India has one hundred and eight (108) million Muslims, approximately 11% of its population. Pakistan, where riots and anti-American demonstrations continue to rage, has one hundred and thirty six (136) million Muslims, 95% of its people. Even if only 1% of that population is made up of rabid fundamentalist radicals, it totals 1.36 million people who stand with Osama bin Laden. It is a great wonder that just 10,000 recently crossed the border to fight with the Taliban.

To the surprise of many people, there is a large Muslim population in China. In fact, nearly thirty (30) million Muslims live in China. The former Soviet Union, the whole Southern tier, along the border with Afghanistan, Iran, Syria and Iraq and all across to Turkey, is home for more than forty-one (41) million Muslims. In Turkey, there are about sixty-two (62) million, 92% of the population and in Iran, sixty-three (63) million Muslims make up 97% of its population and on it goes.

Islam is now the second largest religion in Europe. In Great Britain, there are now over one and a half million Muslims, with some fifteen hundred Mosques. In the United States, thirty years ago, Islam was virtually non-existent. But, because of heavy immigration from Muslim countries, there is now an Islamic population of over six million. Many Muslims have fled the oppression of the Islamic states, seeking freedom in the United States.

Muslim-based sects such as the Nation of Islam (which appeals especially to African-Americans) and Bahai (which proclaims the unity of the human race) have special appeal to many Americans. Islam, itself, is composed of two major divisions — the mainstream Sunni (the largest) and the more radical Shi'ites. The mystical tradition of Sufism includes many Sunnis and some Shi'ites.

A PEOPLE CUT OFF FROM THE CHRISTIAN WORLD VIEW

God gave us a great commission, to go into all the world and proclaim the good news of Jesus Christ. But, sadly to say, we have not carried that great commission, as we should, into the Muslim world. Only two per cent of American missionaries have been involved in Muslim ministries. We have one Christian missionary for every one million Muslims. Islam now represents the single most challenge to Christianity. No matter how peaceful many Muslims are, their core doctrine allows for no other faith to legitimately exist within the borders of its control and influence.

POLITICALLY CORRECT MISINFORMATION

We seem to be bombarded with media reports of how the Muslims in America are beset with fear because we have misinterpreted their faith as one with roots of aggression against Jews and Christians. The media has been waging an information battle against this, proclaiming the Islam is a region of peace and love.

That this is not evident in the many Islamic countries is beside the point. The continual path of murder and death from the Palestinian Hamas' suicide squads proves just the opposite. The pictures of Palestinians rejoicing in the streets, celebrating our tragedy confirms the true heart of the radical Muslim.

Hal Lindsey reported on *www.hallindseyoracle.com* that one Muslim cleric, praying for peace at the National Cathedral, along side our President and many mighty men of God on that Friday Day Of Remembrance, wasn't that patriotic. That same Islamic leader was at a rally in California a few months earlier where they burned an American Flag along with an Israeli one. We must be cautious. While the Islamic leaders of the Middle East were smiling softly at the cameras for CNN and their American audience, they had this to say to their own people, as reported by the Muslim 'Palestinian Times.'

PALESTINIAN SCHOLARS FORBID JOINING AMERICAN CAMPAIGN AGAINST AFGHANISTAN

Occupied Jerusalem – Muslim Ulema (religious scholars) throughout Palestine have issued an edict prohibiting Muslim States from joining the American-led crusade against Afghanistan or any other Muslim countries.

A Fatwah or religious ruling issued recently by the League of Palestinian Ulema, which represents over 500 religious scholars and academics in Palestine, stated that "it is amply clear in light of the Holy Qur'an and the traditions of our Holy Prophet (peace be upon him) that it is inadmissible for Muslims to enter into alliance with non-Muslims against fellow Muslims."

The edict cited evidence from the Qur'an and Sunnah (the

sayings, actions and silences of the Prophet) to that effect. It warned Muslims against falling into the trap of fighting and killing fellow Muslims under the rubric of "fighting terrorism."

Several similar Fatwahs have been issued throughout the Muslim world, all forbidding Muslims from joining the expected American campaign against Afghanistan.

Sheikh Ibrahim Zaid al-Kilani, a prominent Islamic figure in Jordan, had also issued a strongly worded statement admonishing Arab regimes against "joining ranks with the disbelievers against fellow Muslims." He invoked the Qur'anic verse that states, "Whoever joins them (the disbelievers) is one of them." (Palestinian Times, Web Report, October 2001.)

A SEVENTH CENTURY PEOPLE IN A 21ST CENTURY WORLD

To understand Islam, perhaps the key factor is to realize that Islam must be understood in the religious and cultural context of seventh century Arabia.

What Mohammed did was to raise seventh century culture to the status of divine law. In fact, Islam is the deification of seventh century Arabian culture. Unless you understand the historical context of when and where Mohammed was born, you will never understand Islam.

Dr. Arthur Arberry, the head of Mid-Eastern Studies at Cambridge University and one of the great Arabic scholars said:

> "Islam is a peculiarly Arabian religion because Islam is a religion and culture, and as a religion and culture, they are one. It must be understood," he said, "in terms of its essential identification with Seventh Century culture."

Islam imposes its seventh century Arabian culture, in its political expression, in its family affairs, in its dietary laws, in its clothing, in its religious rites, and in its language. They are religiously and socially compelled to impose seventh century Arab culture on the rest of the cultures in the world.

Mohammed took the political laws that governed seventh century Arabian tribes, and literally made them the laws of Allah, their God. In such tribes, the Sheik or chief of the nomadic tribe had absolute authority. There was no concept of civil or personal rights in seventh century Arabia. This is why Islamic countries are inevitably ruled by dictators or strong men who rule as despots. There are twenty-one Arab nations today, and not one of them is a modern democracy.

The more Islamic Fundamentalism gains dominance, the more a nation is plunged back into the dark ages of seventh century Arabia. Iran is a good example of this. The despots today of Libya, Iran, Iraq, Syria, Afghanistan, the Sudan and Yemen are merely examples of such Arabian tyranny grafted into modern times.

Because there was no concept of personal freedom or civil rights in tribal life of seventh century Arabia, Islamic law today does not recognize freedom of speech, freedom of religion, freedom of assembly or freedom of the press. This is why non-Muslims such as Christians, are routinely denied the most basic of human rights, often physically attacked or jailed. These incidents can often be violent.

This conflict is a major reason the modern Arabs have immigrated to the United States in such numbers. It often comes at a great cost, including family alienation. We need to understand and have compassion for them.

CHRISTIANS ARE AMONG THE INFIDELS OF ISLAM

In Indonesia – (From Sunday, Jan.3, 1993, Washington Post), crowds of Muslims were reacting to what they regarded as proselytizing by Christians, attacked or burned several Christian churches or homes on the islands of Java and Sumatra. In the biggest reported incident, more than ten thousand Muslims, apparently well organized, tore down and burned the home of a Christian preacher outside Perusia, a town in East Java, to protest tracts that he was distributing.

The mob then wrecked two nearby Protestant churches, unconnected to the preacher. The head of Indonesia's largest Islamic organization says at least thirty attacks on churches or other Christian property were reported in the previous three months.

In the Philippines – The Associated Press, reported on 2/8/93, that: "Western human rights groups say that a quick mobilization by their international networks may have saved the lives of two Christian Philippine leaders, imprisoned in Saudi Arabia."

Reliable sources within the human rights community reported that two lay pastors scheduled to be executed on Christmas Day by the government of Saudi Arabia were arrested in October and charged with violating kingdom law by preaching Christianity. The two had apparently been in hiding since January when a Christian service they led in a private home, was raided by Saudi religious police. Reports of the scheduled execution prompted a flurry of international inquiries and protests, including a harshly worded appeal to King Faud from Philippine president, Fidel Ramos".

These efforts were futile. They were beheaded in Saudi Arabia because they dared to hold a Christian Bible study.

In Saudi Arabia – This is the same country where Christians by the tens of thousands had just stood in defense of its soil against attacks from Iraq. There is no freedom of religion in Saudi Arabia. In fact, one of the biggest tragedies of the Gulf War was that when we sent our men over there to fight on the behalf of Saudi Arabia, our Christian chaplains weren't even allowed to wear their little crosses on their lapels. The government of Saudi Arabia said they were not allowed to hold Christian chapel services for our soldiers who were protecting their country. Service personnel were advised to leave their

Bibles at home. This was because Islamic law that forbids any presence or mention of Christianity.

In the Sudan – Washington Post, 1/13/93, "Sudan's radical Islam regime is not just waging a genocidal war in the South against Christians, it is also part of a larger Islamic push. It made itself a training ground for Islamic terrorists to overthrow Egypt's pro-Western regime. For months now, Islamic terrorists have been going around and randomly shooting foreign tourists in an attempt to kill the major foreign currency earner of a desperately poor country so that they might be turned back to the Islamic laws.

THE WOMEN OF ISLAM
One of the most demeaning practices of Islam is its barbaric treatment of women. Women are considered property in the fundamental sects of Islam. They are not allowed to have ownership of any kind of property. Approximately 75% of Muslim women suffer female circumcision in a most barbaric, painful ritual designed to make them obedient and docile. They are dressed from head to toe in clothes that cover all but the eyes and often these are covered by a veil. Their illiteracy rate is higher than 75%.

It is interesting that what an illiterate nomadic tribeswoman wore in the desert in seventh century Arabia is still mandated as the dress code for Muslim women today. It's a denial of civil rights to women and is reflective of the Islamic Arabian culture and its low view of women. Today, Muslim men still have the right to have up to 4 wives and while polygamy has been a crime on the United States for over a century, many Muslims here quietly practice it without a word from the authorities.

While the democratic nations have openly accepted the people of the Islamic faith within our countries and have encouraged them to worship freely, as they desire, the same is not true in their own countries. You might remember what took place during the Gulf War. On March 10, 1991, The New York Times magazine reported the following story about women's rights in Saudi Arabia.

The crisis in the Gulf War has spawned a messy and much publicized demonstration by women who dumped their chauffeurs and drove in convoy, defying a ban on women driving in Saudi Arabia. The incident prompted a vicious campaign against them by religious fanatics with government acquiescence. Underlying these strains is the question of how much power the religious establishment should have, in particular, the religious police who patrol the streets and shopping malls, telling the women to cover their faces, and young men to pray. The only people with spine in their society were forty-seven women who drove, one Saudi intellectual has said. And look what happened to them. They were thrown to the wolves. The government punished them as severely as it would any public protester. Virtually all those who taught (school) were dismissed by order of the King.

The women, as well as their husbands, were forbidden to leave the kingdom. They were forbidden to speak with foreign reporters or to discuss their situation with an outsider. They were warned of further reprisals if they attempted to drive again and stage another demonstration. It makes you wonder what we were trying to defend over in Saudi Arabia.

But the government's treatment of these women was mild compared to their treatment by the Islamic religious establishment. The fundamentalist sheiks denounced them from one of the kingdom's most powerful political platforms, the Mosque Opus.

In the Friday services after the demonstration the women were branded as *"red communists, dirty American secularists, whores and prostitutes, fallen women and advocators of vice"*. Their names, occupations, addresses and phone numbers were distributed in leaflets at the mosques and other public places. One leaflet accused them of having denounced Islam, an offense punishable by death in Saudi Arabia. And these women, folks, were all educated PhDs, with most of them teaching at the University there. Some were medical doctors. They were threatened with death. What had they done? They had gotten into cars and drove them. Several of the women remained unrepentant; convinced eventually the issue of their status will be addressed. "The issue is not driving," one of them said." It is that here in Saudi Arabia I exist as a person only from the belly button to the knees."

THE GODS OF THE SEVENTH CENTURY

The culture of Mohammed's world was very animistic. Every Arab tribe had its sacred magic stone(s) that they believed protected the tribe, resident in the Kaaba. Mohammed's particular tribe had adopted a black stone and had set it in the Kaaba. This magical black stone was kissed when people came on their pilgrimages and worshipped at the Kaaba. It was probably an asteroid or a meteorite, a moonstone, which they viewed as being divine. All the nomadic tribes had their own tribal deities.

The dominant religion just prior to Mohammed was Sabianism, a religion in which heavenly bodies were worshipped. The moon was viewed as a male deity, and they used a lunar calendar. Their pagan rite of fasting began with the appearance of the crescent moon. Fasting was later adopted as one of the five pillars of faith of Islam. Fasting, based on the lunar calendar, in the ninth month of Ramadan already pre-existed in the Arab culture before Mohammed was even born.

What about the name "Allah?" Muslims claim that Allah is the same God as Christians worship, just under another name. Yet, if you look at the history of it, it is very different. The term "Allah" is a purely Arabic term used in reference to an Arabian deity. The tribe into which Mohammed was born was particularly devoted to their Allah, which was the moon god. It was represented by the black stone they believed had come down from heaven.

In Arabia, the sun god was viewed as female and the moon was viewed as the male god. In pre-Islamic times, Allah, the moon god, was married to the sun god, and together they produced three goddesses called The Daughters of Allah. They were viewed as being at the top of the pantheon of Arabian deities, those three hundred and sixty idols in the Kaaba, at Mecca. Do not ever accept Allah as just another name of the true and living God, the God of Abraham, Isaac and Jacob. This Arabian deity was the god of the Ishmaelites. Ishmael was not the son of the covenant. Isaac was the son of the covenant.

The symbol of the worship of the moon god, Allah, in pre-Islamic Arab culture, throughout the Middle East, was the crescent moon. Today, the crescent moon is on every flag of an Islamic nation. Go to any mosque. What is on top of it? A crescent moon, the symbol of Allah, the moon god. Every Muslim nation that has a flag has a crescent moon on the flag.

Mohammed, the prophet of Islam, was born in 570 A.D. and lived for sixty-two years, dying in 632. At the time he was born, Mecca was the center of trade and religious activity. Mohammed was a camel driver until the age of twenty-five when he met and married a lady who was fifteen years his senior. She was forty years old, a wealthy lady.

For the next fifteen years, he ran the family fruit business in Mecca. It wasn't until he was forty years old that he began to receive his revelations. He would go, as seekers of truth would, up to a cave that was about three miles north of Mecca to pray and meditate.

THE VISITATION OF GABRIEL
According to Muslim tradition, it was in this cave that the angel Gabriel came to Mohammed. Actually there are four different statements of what happened (in the Koran) which contradict each other. The Muslims say that it was Gabriel, and they took

this as a sign that Mohammed was the true prophet to the Arabs.

After meditating there, off and on for two years, Muslims say that Mohammed received revelations, during which he would go into epileptic fits. That's what Muslims believe they were. He would shake, he would perspire, and he would foam at the mouth. Whether they were epileptic or even demonic, he claimed that during these fits, he received revelations from an angel of light, which he claimed was Gabriel.

What were the revelations? They were written down into what is known as the Koran, the Islamic scripture or holy book. They were not written down until years later because Mohammed was uneducated and probably did not know how to write or read.

The main message that Mohammed communicated was that there was no god but Allah, that he was the one true god who created everything. The second thing he taught was that man is God's slave, and it is his first duty to submit to God and to obey him. The term Islam, in Arabic, means submission, and a Muslim is one who submits to the will of Allah. Mohammed said the chief duty of man is to submit to the will of Allah.

Third, he said there is coming a great and terrible day of judgment in which God will raise up the dead to life and will judge them and reward them, based upon their deeds. Those who were found worthy would be given to a wonderful, sensuous life in heaven, and those who do not make it will be condemned to hell.

The majority of the people at Mecca did not think too highly of this new Prophet and his revelations. They began to criticize and attack him. In 622 A.D. he fled to Medina, about two hundred and eighty miles north of Mecca. This was the beginning of Islam.

THE AGE OF ISLAM BEGINS

In the Middle East, everything is based upon the time that Mohammed fled to Medina in 622 A.D. That's the beginning of their calendar; zero, in the Muslim calendar.

It was in Medina that he first tried to get the Christians and Jews who were living there to follow him as "the prophet." He called himself a prophet and an apostle, although that term was not used in their culture. He used the term "prophet" to appeal to the Jews and "apostle" to appeal to the Christians.

He told them, interestingly, to pray to Jerusalem. When they did not accept him as a prophet or an apostle, he then rejected them and told the other people to pray to Mecca to Allah, his tribal deity. He then began to receive more revelations. It is very interesting what these revelations were. He received revelations that he was to loot and steal from caravans that were going through. There were many cases where Mohammed and his followers would loot and rob caravans and would kill the men in order to satisfy his greed. In fact, the Koran and history reports that he fought over sixty-six such battles, killing tens of thousands.

In one of his revelations, he was told to kill and drive out all the Jews. On one occasion, he had one thousand Jewish men brought together and had them all beheaded. Islam became known as the religion of the sword. In 628 A.D., Mohammed received a revelation that Islam was to be exalted above all other religions including Christianity and Judaism.

In 629 A.D. Mohammed raised up an army of ten thousand men. He returned to Mecca and conquered Mecca where he had been raised. By force, he imposed Islam on the rest of the Arabian tribes. He died in 632 A.D. having conquered much of the Arabian Peninsula. Islam then spread, by the sword, across North Africa, and for 14 centuries has continued converting by the sword in its reign of terror and intimidation.

THE SIX BELIEFS OF ISLAM

1. **God**: There is one true God, named Allah.

2. **Angels:** They are the servants of God, through whom he reveals his will. The greatest angel is Gabriel who appeared to Mohammed. Everyone has two "recording angels": one to record their good deeds, the other to record their bad deeds.

3. **The Prophets:** Allah has spoken through many prophets, but the final and greatest of these is Mohammed. Other prophets include Noah, Abraham, Moses and Jesus.

4. **The Holy Books:** The Koran or Qur'an is the holiest book of Islam, believed to be Allah's final revelation to man and it supersedes all previous revelations, including the Bible. It contains Allah's word as passed on orally to Mohammed by Gabriel. It contains 114 chapters or Suras *(also called Surahs.. I will use the word Sura for Chapter here)*. It is pure and without error. Muslims also recognize the Law of Moses, the Psalms and the gospels but consider them to be badly corrupted.

    The Hadith or Sunnah contains the recorded sayings and deeds of the prophet Mohammed. It is second only to the Koran and is often used to clarify things not clear in the Koran.

5. **The Day of Judgment:** A terrible day on which each person's good and bad deeds will be balanced to determine his fate. Muslims will go to paradise and all nonbelievers and Muslims who did not maintain their faith and good works will go to hell. There is no original sin. All of mankind starts out of sinless, thus the need for a final judgment.

6. **The Decree of God:** Allah ordains the fate of all. Muslims are fatalistic. "If Allah, wills it" is the comment of a devout Muslim on almost every situation or decision he faces.

THE FIVE PILLARS OF ISLAM

1. **Affirmation:** "There is no God but Allah and Mohammed is his messenger" which is recited constantly by devout Muslims.
2. **The Fast:** Faithful Muslims fast from dawn to dusk every day during the ninth month of the Islamic calendar, Ramadan, which is sacred.
3. **Almsgiving:** A worthy Muslim must give 2.5% of his income to the poor.
4. **Prayer:** Muslims are required to pray five times a day, kneeling and facing Mecca.
5. **The Pilgrimage:** Muslims are expected to journey to Mecca at least once in their lifetime.

ISLAM AND CHRISTIANITY COMPARED

ISLAM IS ONE OF THOSE "OTHER gospels" that Paul warned us about time and again. In Chapter 11 of II Corinthians, Paul warns us that Satan himself transforms himself into an angel of light. Islam teaches that God is so far above man in every way that he is virtually unknowable. He will send individuals to Paradise or Hell as they deserve and as he chooses.

WHAT THE KORAN SAYS ABOUT JESUS
He was not the Son of God.

> And the Jews say: Uzair is the son of Allah; and the Christians say: The Messiah is the son of Allah; these are the words of their mouths; they imitate the saying of those

who disbelieved before; may Allah destroy them; how they are turned away! (Sura 9:30)

He was not divine.

Certainly they disbelieve who say: Surely, Allah— He is the Messiah, son of Marium. Say: Who then could control anything as against Allah when He wished to destroy the Messiah son of Marium and his mother and all those on the earth? And Allah's is the kingdom of the heavens and the earth and what is between them; He creates what He pleases; and Allah has power over all things. (Sura 5.17)

The Messiah, son of Marium is but an apostle; apostles before him have indeed passed away; and his mother was a truthful woman; they both used to eat food. See how We make the communications clear to them, then behold, how they are turned away. (Sura 5.75)

He was not crucified.

And their saying: Surely we have killed the Messiah, Isa son of Marium, the apostle of Allah; and they did not kill him nor did they crucify him, but it appeared to them so (like Isa) and most surely those who differ therein are only in a doubt about it; they have no knowledge respecting it, but only follow a conjecture, and they killed him not for sure. (Sura 4.157)

Nay! Allah took him up to Himself; and Allah is Mighty, Wise. (Sura 4.15)

He did not atone for our sins.

On the day when the earth shall be changed into a different earth, and the heavens (as well), and they shall come forth before Allah, the One, the Supreme. And you will see the guilty on that day linked together in chains. Their shirts made of pitch and the fire covering their faces. That Allah may requite each soul (according to) what it has earned; surely Allah is swift in reckoning. (Sura14.48-51)

He will return but His second Coming is to be a witness for Mohammed. "

> And there is not one of the followers of the Book but most certainly believes in this before his death, and on the day of resurrection he (Isa) shall be a witness against them. (Sura 4.159)

He is not God come in the flesh, the 'son' of God. There is no Trinity.

> O followers of the Book! do not exceed the limits in your religion, and do not speak (lies) against Allah, but (speak) the truth; the Messiah, Isa son of Marium is only an apostle of Allah and His Word which He communicated to Marium and a spirit from Him; believe therefore in Allah and His apostles, and say not, Three. Desist, it is better for you; Allah is only one God; far be It from His glory that He should have a son, whatever is in the heavens and whatever is in the earth is His, and Allah is sufficient for a Protector. (Sura 4.171)

> Certainly they disbelieve who say: Surely Allah is the third (person) of the three; and there is no god but the one God, and if they desist not from what they say, a painful chastisement shall befall those among them who disbelieve. (Sura 5.73)

WHAT THE BIBLE SAYS ABOUT JESUS

> *In the beginning was the Word, and the Word was with God, and the Word was God. He was with God in the beginning. Through him all things were made; without him nothing was made that has been made. In him was life, and that life was the light of men.*

> *The Word became flesh and made his dwelling among us. We have seen his glory, the glory of the One and Only, who came from the Father, full of grace and truth. (John 1:1 -4, 14)*

> *For God so loved the world that he gave his one and only Son, that whoever believes in him shall not perish but have eternal life. (John 3:16)*

Jesus answered, "I am the way and the truth and the life. No one comes to the Father except through me." (John 14:6).

Dear friends, do not believe every spirit, but test the spirits to see whether they are from God, because many false prophets have gone out into the world. This is how you can recognize the Spirit of God: Every spirit that acknowledges that Jesus Christ has come in the flesh is from God, but every spirit that does not acknowledge Jesus is not from God. This is the spirit of the antichrist, which you have heard is coming and even now is already in the world. (1 John 4:1 - 3)

For in Christ all the fullness of the Deity lives in bodily form. (Colosians 2:9)

This is my blood of the covenant, which is poured out for many for the forgiveness of sins. (Matthew 26: 28)

When he had received the drink, Jesus said, "It is finished." With that, he bowed his head and gave up his spirit. (John 19:30)

Many of the Jews read this sign, for the place where Jesus was crucified was near the city, and the sign was written in Aramaic, Latin and Greek. (John 19:20)

In the past God spoke to our forefathers through the prophets at many times and in various ways, but in these last days he has spoken to us by his Son, whom he appointed heir of all things, and through whom he made the universe. The Son is the radiance of God's glory and the exact representation of his being, sustaining all things by his powerful word. After he had provided purification for sins, he sat down at the right hand of the Majesty in heaven. (Hebrews 1: 1-3)

A DIFFERENT GOD?

Is Allah, this stone idol, the God of Abraham, Isaac and Jacob? Just because Mohammed said so doesn't make it so! Allah chose Hagar and her son, Ishmael for his covenant. The God of the Bible chose Abraham's other son, Isaac, as heir to His covenant. This act has forever separated the two and the people of Ishmael have warred against the children of Isaac ever since.

> And the Angel of the LORD said to her (Hagar): "Behold, you are with child, and you shall bear a son. You shall call his name Ishmael, because the LORD has heard your affliction. He shall be a wild man; his hand shall be against every man, and every man's hand against him. And he shall dwell in the presence of all his brethren." *(Genesis 16:11-12)*
>
> And Abraham said to God, "If only Ishmael might live under your blessing!" Then God said, "Yes, but your wife Sarah will bear you a son, and you will call him Isaac. I will establish my covenant with him as an everlasting covenant for his descendants after him.
>
> "And as for Ishmael, I have heard you: I will surely bless him; I will make him fruitful and will greatly increase his numbers. He will be the father of twelve rulers, and I will make him into a great nation.
>
> "But my covenant I will establish with Isaac, whom Sarah will bear to you by this time next year." When he had finished speaking with Abraham, God went up from him." *(Genesis 17:18 - 22)*

Allah is an impersonal being, impossible to approach or comprehend. The Bible's God befriends men like Abraham (Isaiah 41:8) and talks with them (Genesis 18:23-33)! He loved us so much He sent His only begotten Son to die for us (John 3:16)!

Allah is a god of fear and terrorism that commands destruction upon those who refuse to convert to Islam. The Bible's God delights to show His boundless mercy. His gospel is the "Good News" of peace and forgiveness.

Allah requires total obedience to Islam and weighs the works of people. Allah and the Koran relegate Jesus to just the last prophet before Mohammed, below his authority. Jesus was not the Way, and could only point the way to Mohammed. The Bible clearly states that *Jesus was and still is the way*.

Allah required the works of Mohammed to complete his words of judgment to man. The God of The Bible sent His son who did the finished work of grace for man.

In the light of Allah's actual origin and his radical difference from the God of the Bible, we must conclude that Allah is not God. Nor is the name, Allah, a generic Mid-East name for God, as even many Christians think. Allah is the name of a false god who cannot save anyone from anything. Rather, through his false prophet, Mohammed, he continues to lead hundreds of millions into eternal darkness.

IT'S A MYSTERY TO ME

IT IS A REAL MYSTERY TO ME HOW THE ISLAMIC WORLD PERCEIVES JESUS...

IN ISLAM, WE ARE TOLD HE was born of God, not man, lived a pure and sinless life, was not crucified, but raised to heaven and shall come again to proclaim Mohammed the greatest prophet and Islam the true faith. He will tell the entire world that he was here to really proclaim the coming of Mohammed. He will say that the Jews, his disciples and all of Christendom have been wrong for two thousand years, and we must all convert to Islam to be saved.

Yet, if we follow this through, we come to some strange conclusions.

1. If what they say about his birth, life, ministry and bodily accession to heaven are true, then we have to ask why this would be. If the second part of this picture is true, his submission to Mohammed, the one mightier than he, why would he say so many things like, *"I am the way and the truth and the life. No one comes to the Father except through me."* (John 14:6) or *"I and My Father are one." (Then the Jews took up stones again to stone Him)* (John 10:30-31).

2. Why would he foretell his death on the cross and his resurrection from death? Either the Koran is wrong or the Bible is wrong and Jesus was a liar. If he was a liar, how could the Koran say he lived a sinless life and was lifted up to heaven by God? There can be no compromise in such a black or white issue. He was either who he said he was or the greatest liar in history. The Muslims cannot have it both ways in such a basic matter. A thing cannot 'be' and 'not be' at the same time.

3. If the Muslim view of Christ were true, why would we read about John being the proclaimer of the coming Christ, when we should be reading about Jesus proclaiming the coming of Mohammed? *(Some Islamic scholars interpret verses foretelling the coming of the Holy Spirit to mean the coming of Mohammed).*

4. If Mohammed was the greater, why was Jesus (the liar) lifted up to heaven and Mohammed left to die and be buried like every other man? I am reminded of the scripture in the 82nd Chapter of the book of Psalms, where the unrighteous rulers and judges were rebuked for their evil doings and self – exaltation. *"They do not know, nor do they understand; they walk about in darkness; all the foundations of the earth are unstable. I said, "You are gods, and all of you are children of the Most High. But you shall die like men, and fall like one of the princes."*

A FEW IMPORTANT QUESTIONS TO ASK YOUR MUSLIM FRIENDS

EVEN IN ISLAMIC DOCTRINE, SOME KEY issues of the lives of Christ and Mohammed do not make sense. Jesus was born of God, by a virgin, Mohammed was born of man; Jesus lived a life of purity, without sin, history shows that Mohammed did not; Jesus healed the sick, opened blind eyes, healed the lepers, raised the dead, walked on water, quieted the raging sea, Mohammed did none of these things; Jesus was raised to heaven, glorified by the father, Mohammed died a man and was buried as any other man. Jesus will fulfill his prophetic promise of coming again; Mohammed made no such claim.

THE HOLY JIHAD ~ A WAY OF LIFE AND DEATH

350 MUSLIM SCHOLARS CONFIRM LEGITIMACY OF MARTYRDOM OPERATIONS.

Baghdad – As many as 350 Muslim religious scholars meeting in Baghdad have confirmed in the strongest terms the legitimacy of martyrdom operations as one of the highest forms of Jihad against oppression.

The scholars unanimously concluded after three days of deliberations that Palestinian Mujahideen, or freedom fighters, who blow themselves up at enemy targets are not suicidal but are bona fide martyrs whose acts are totally compatible with Islamic teachings.

"It is the duty of every Muslim facing overwhelming and brutal aggression, as is the case in Palestine, to confront this oppression with all available means," said the scholars in their edict.

The edict reaffirmed previous edicts by such prominent Islamic jurists as Sheikh Yousef al-Qaradawi, who ruled that freedom fighters who detonate explosives strapped to themselves sacrifice their lives to attack the "enemies of God and Islam."

"The people of Palestine have been forced into a situation where they must choose between dying as martyr-bombers or slaughtered like sheep at the hands of a nefarious enemy.

Dying as martyr-bombers in this case is considered a very sublime form of Jihad," said the edict.

Martyrdom operations, which the Jewish-controlled media in the U.S. and Europe refer to as "suicide bomb attacks," have attracted overwhelming support among Muslim theologians, particularly after Palestinian Islamist leaders explained that martyrdom operations were the only means to make the Jews refrain from perpetrating a large-scale holocaust against Palestinian civilians.

This point was also illustrated during the Baghdad conference and reportedly received unanimous approval from participating scholars.

A few months ago, the U.S. exerted behind-the-curtain pressure on the Saudi government to instruct the Saudi religious establishment to issue edicts opposing martyrdom operations. However, many Saudi scholars rejected American pressure to that effect, describing American intervention in "Islamic theological matters as brazen and shameless." (The Palestinian Times, on Line, October 2001 Report)

WHAT'S IT ALL ABOUT?

The Jihad is a holy war, one fought to the death, a great and noble death honoring Allah in the defensive of the faith. Those who die as martyrs of the faith receive immediate entrance to heaven, where they are given many virgins and opulent mansions filled with wealth and servants for their great gift to the cause of Allah. This cause is the slaying of those who will not live the peace of Islam, those who have brought strife against the children of Allah.

> O you who believe! Shall I guide you to a commerce that will save you from a painful torment? That you believe in Allah and His Messenger and that you strive hard and fight in the Cause of Allah with your wealth and your lives, that will be better for you, if you but know! (If you do so) He will forgive you your sins, and admit you into Gardens under

which rivers flow, and pleasant dwelling in Gardens of
Eternity, that is indeed the great success. (Sura 61: 10-12)

Islamic clerics on TV by the scores are claiming that the jihad and destruction such as seen on 9/11/01 is not part of the Muslim faith. They speak about 'The Peace of Islam" or "The Peace of Allah," terms that sound fine in simple English, but actually mean being at peace by converting and bowing to Allah alone. Anyone outside that narrow definition is among the Infidels.

Unfortunately, the Jihad is a very real, core element of the Islamic faith. It is also a doctrinal teaching that has led to the deaths of millions of Muslims throughout history. Let's look at the Holy Jihad being waged against America. It is not just a single group of militants. That would make our work easy. This Jihad is operating across the entire world of Islam and draws its fanatics from every corner of the faith.

I was exchanging e-mails with several Muslims as I worked through this report and in discussing the attempt to separate Islam out from the terrorist attacks, one scoffed at such an idea. He wrote:

> Islam does not compartmentalize life into the so-called sacred and secular. Get this clear. Life is one unit. Not clear enough? In Islam it is not possible to disentangle the spiritual from the political or the cultural from the economic. Islam is the path of unification and a total way of life. Everything that Muslims do is unified with Islam.

Hal Lindsey is one of the most knowledgeable Christians on this subject, having studied Islam and Muslims for many years. In His daily commentary at his web site, www.hallindseyoracle.com, he had this to say on 9/17/01:

> The enemy we face is far more than a certain country, or a certain race. It is multi-national and multi-racial. The enemy is found all over the world disguised in many clever guises. The enemy is organized into cell groups that can operate autonomously or can be joined into multi-cell

strike groups, as on September the 11th. The enemy is fanatical and totally dedicated to the common goal of destroying the USA and Israel.

Our enemy has been created by one common all consuming core-Islam. Our enemy is blindly courageous because of the teachings of his religious leaders that when he dies attacking the enemy, he goes immediately to paradise to be given 70 beautiful virgins for his heavenly harem. Our enemy will therefore gladly volunteer to give his life in a suicide attack against the USA and its people.

All the forces of Fundamental Islam have not just declared war on the USA; they have declared a "Jihad or holy war" against us. This Jihad has been strengthened with many "Fatwahs", which give specific, murderous and explicit religious commands to kill all Americans in every place and by any means possible.

Osama bin Laden issued such a Fatwah in which he declared it to be the sacred duty to Allah for all Muslims to kill Americans at every opportunity by any means. Specifically, his Fatwah ordered, "We, with God's help call on every Muslim who believes in God and wishes to be rewarded to comply with God's order to kill the Americans and plunder their money wherever and whenever they find it.

That is who bin-Laden's enemy is. It isn't the United States. It isn't the government. It is each and every individual American — ordinary Americans like those who now lie entombed under a million tons of rubble in Manhattan. It's you.

YES, THIS IS ABOUT ISLAM
Salman Rushdie has been on a death list ever since he wrote a less than spiritual book about his faith. He has been in hiding for years now. These are some of his comments about this holy war that isn't a holy war. They are excerpted from article published by him in The New York Times, on November 2, 2001.

LONDON – "This isn't about Islam." The world's leaders have been repeating this mantra for weeks, partly in the virtuous hope of deterring reprisal attacks on innocent Muslims living in the West, partly because if the United States is to maintain its coalition against terror it can't afford to suggest that Islam and terrorism are in any way related.

The trouble with this necessary disclaimer is that it isn't true. If this isn't about Islam, why the worldwide Muslim demonstrations in support of Osama bin Laden and Al Qaeda? Why did those 10,000 men armed with swords and axes mass on the Pakistan-Afghanistan frontier, answering some mullah's call to jihad? Why are the war's first British casualties three Muslim men who died fighting on the Taliban side?

Why the routine anti-Semitism of the much-repeated Islamic slander that "the Jews" arranged the hits on the World Trade Center and the Pentagon, with the oddly self-deprecating explanation offered by the Taliban leadership, among others, that Muslims could not have the technological know-how or organizational sophistication to pull off such a feat? Why does Imran Khan, the Pakistani ex-sports star turned politician, demand to be shown the evidence of Al Qaeda's guilt while apparently turning a deaf ear to the self-incriminating statements of Al Qaeda's own spokesmen (there will be a rain of aircraft from the skies, Muslims in the West are warned not to live or work in tall buildings)? Why all the talk about American military infidels desecrating the sacred soil of Saudi Arabia if some sort of definition of what is sacred is not at the heart of the present discontents?

Of course this is "about Islam." The question is, what exactly does that mean? After all, most religious belief isn't very theological. Most Muslims are not profound Koranic analysts. For a vast number of "believing" Muslim men, "Islam" stands, in a jumbled, half-examined way, not only for the fear of God — the fear more than the love, one suspects — but also for a cluster of customs, opinions and prejudices that include their dietary practices; the sequestration or near-sequestration of "their" women; the sermons delivered by their mullahs of choice; a loathing of modern society in general, riddled as it is with music, godlessness and sex; and a more particularized loathing (and fear) of the prospect that their own immediate surroundings could be taken over — "Westoxicated" — by the liberal Western-style way of life.

These Islamists — we must get used to this word, "Islamists," meaning those who are engaged upon such political projects, and learn to distinguish it from the more general and politically neutral "Muslim" — include the Muslim Brotherhood in Egypt, the blood-soaked combatants of the Islamic Salvation Front and Armed Islamic Group in Algeria, the Shiite revolutionaries of Iran, and the Taliban. Poverty is their great helper, and the fruit of their efforts is paranoia. This paranoid Islam, which blames outsiders, "infidels," for all the ills of Muslim societies, and whose proposed remedy is the closing of those societies to the rival project of modernity, is presently the fastest growing version of Islam in the world.

IS THIS JIHAD REALLY AN ISLAMIC DOCTRINE?
Let's read what the Koran, the Islamic Holy Scriptures, says:

> And those who perform jihad for Us, We shall certainly guide them in Our ways, and God is surely with the doers of good. (Sura 29: 69)

> O you who believe! Shall I guide you to a commerce that will save you from a painful torment. That you believe in Allah and His Messenger and that you strive hard and fight in the Cause of Allah with your wealth and your lives, that will be better for you, if you but know! (If you do so) He will forgive you your sins, and admit you into Gardens under which rivers flow, and pleasant dwelling in Gardens of Eternity, that is indeed the great success. (Sura 61: 10-12)

> O you who believe! Do not take the Jews and the Christians for friends; they are friends of each other; and whoever

amongst you takes them for a friend, then surely he is one of them; surely Allah does not guide the unjust people. Your friend can be only Allah; and His messenger and those who believe.

O you who believe! do not take for guardians those who take your religion for a mockery and a joke, from among those who were given the Book before you and the unbelievers; and be careful of (your duty to) Allah if you are believers. (Sura 5:51, 57)

The punishment of those who wage war against Allah and His Apostle and strive to make mischief in the land is only this, that they should be murdered or crucified or their hands and their feet should be cut off on opposite sides or they should be imprisoned; this shall be as a disgrace for them in this world, and in the hereafter they shall have a grievous chastisement. (Sura 5:33)

So when the sacred months have passed away, then slay the idolaters wherever you find them, and take them captives and besiege them and lie in wait for them in every ambush, then if they repent and keep up prayer and pay the poor-rate, leave their way free to them; surely Allah is forgiving, Merciful. (Sura 9:5)

O Prophet! Strive hard against the unbelievers and the hypocrites and be unyielding to them; and their abode is hell, and evil is the destination. (Sura 9:73)

O you who believe! Fight those of the unbelievers who are near to you and let them find you in hardness; and know that Allah is with those who guard (against evil). (Sura 9:123)

And fight with them until there is no more persecution and religion should be only for Allah, but if they desist, then surely Allah sees what they do. (Sura 8:39)

You shall prepare for them all the power you can muster, and all the equipment you can mobilize, that you may frighten the enemies of GOD, your enemies, as well as others who are not known to you; GOD knows them.

Whatever you spend in the cause of GOD will be repaid to you generously, without the least injustice. If they resort to peace, so shall you, and put your trust in GOD. He is the Hearer, the Omniscient. (Sura 8:60-61)

WHAT DOES THE HADITH SAY ABOUT JIHAD?

The Prophet said, "The person who participates in (Holy battles) in Allah's cause and nothing compels him to do so except belief in Allah and His Apostles, will be recompensed by Allah either with a reward, or booty (if he survives) or will be admitted to Paradise (if he is killed in the battle as a martyr). Had I not found it difficult for my followers, then I would not remain behind any sariya going for Jihad and I would have loved to be martyred in Allah's cause and then made alive, and then martyred and then made alive, and then again martyred in His cause." (Vol. 1, Book 2, Number 35. Narrated by Abu Huraira)

Allah's Apostle said, "A pious slave gets a double reward." Abu Huraira added: "By Him in Whose Hands my soul is but for Jihad (i.e. holy battles), Hajj, and my duty to serve my mother, I would have loved to die as a slave." (Volume 3, Book 46, Number 724.Narrated by Abu Huraira)

Allah's Apostle said, "Allah guarantees him who strives in His Cause and whose motivation for going out is nothing but Jihad in His Cause and belief in His Word, that He will admit him into Paradise (if martyred) or bring him back to his dwelling place, whence he has come out, with what he gains of reward and booty." (Volume 9, Book 93, Number 555. Narrated by Abu Huraira)

THE GLORY OF MARTYRDOM – A HOLY DEATH

The Islamic Jihad recruits young Muslims by means of religious indoctrination and bases its terror strategy on the willingness of these young people to lay down their lives for what they see as a divine command — the war against the infidels. Many of the Jihad's terrorist attacks are designed as suicide operations, in which the terrorist attempts to cause as many casualties as possible without planning his own escape. These young men are taken captive by the rhetoric and fanaticism of their religious leaders and the complacency of their governments who either agree with this barbaric level of religious zeal or stand to the side out of fear of angering them.

A CALL TO ARMS

I LOVE THAT GREAT OLD HYMN THAT GOES LIKE THIS:

Onward, Christian soldiers, marching as to war,
with the cross of Jesus going on before.
Christ, the royal Master, leads against the foe;
forward into battle see his banners go!
Onward, Christian soldiers, marching as to war,
with the cross of Jesus going on before.
At the sign of triumph Satan's host doth flee;
on then, Christian soldiers, on to victory!
Hell's foundations quiver at the shout of praise;
brothers, lift your voices, loud your anthems raise.

Let's praise the Lord we are here in such a time of need, a time to be that hand extended, that ambassador in bonds, that one sent forth to be the representative of Christ Jesus. Let our every prayer, our every action be one that would please Him. Pray longer, deeper and with all your prayers, supplications and actions, glorify Him.

Lest we forget – America remains America! God bless our country and our heroes.

FINALLY, BRETHREN

A WORD OF SOUND ADVICE

And whereas it is the duty of nations as well as of men, to own their dependence upon the overruling power of God, to confess their sins and transgressions, in humble sorrow, yet with assured hope that genuine repentance will lead to mercy and pardon; and to recognize the sublime truth, announced in the Holy Scriptures and proven by all history, that those nations only are blessed whose God is the Lord.

And, insomuch as we know that, by His divine law, nations like individuals are subjected to punishments and chastisements in this world, may we not justly fear that the awful calamity of civil war, which now desolates the land, may be but a punishment, inflicted upon us, for our presumptuous sins, to the needful end of our national reformation as a whole People?

We have been the recipients of the choicest bounties of Heaven. We have been preserved, these many years, in peace and prosperity. We have grown in numbers, wealth and power, as no other nation has ever grown. But we have forgotten God. We have forgotten the gracious hand which preserved us in peace, and multiplied and enriched and strengthened us; and we have vainly imagined, in the deceitfulness of our hearts, that all these blessings were produced by some superior wisdom and virtue of our own. Intoxicated with unbroken success, we have become too self-sufficient to feel the necessity of redeeming and preserving grace, too proud to pray to the God that made us! It behooves us then, to humble ourselves before the offended Power, to confess our national sins, and to pray for clemency and forgiveness.

– Abraham Lincoln, 30 March 1863

For further information, contact Ed Decker, Saints Alive in Jesus at ed@SaintsAlive.com or visit our website at www.SaintsAlive.com.

ABOUT THE AUTHOR

Ed Decker is the founder and International Director of Saints Alive in Jesus, a ministry that actively brings the gospel of grace to those lost in the darkness of cultic bondage. An accredited, long time Christian apologist, he is the author of such books as *The God Makers, Decker's Complete Handbook on Mormonism, Fast Facts on False Teachings, To Moroni With Love* and *The Question of Freemasonry*.

For over 30 years, Ed has been an active speaker and teacher, traveling throughout the world working with churches of every Christian denomination. He personally conducts equipping sessions with pastors and lay workers and speaks at conferences in many nations. His ministry extends to radio, television, Christian documentary films and national talk shows.

Ed is a retired pastor and regularly visits hospitals and homes to pray for the sick, counseling and encouraging the body of Christ.

MORE BOOKS FROM ED DECKER

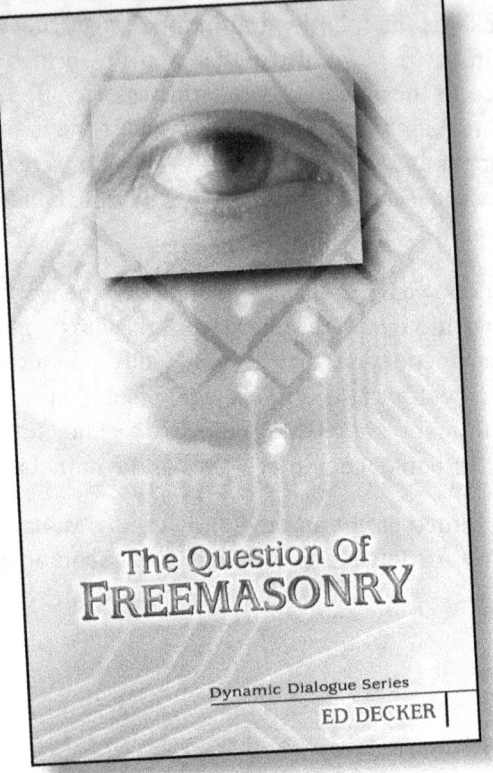

THE QUESTION OF FREEMASONRY
by ED DECKER

Ed's expanded edition of the small book that rocked Masonry. This is one to read and give to your pastor. Masonry is one of the most volatile subjects in the Christian church today. Ed Decker has carefully researched and studied the issues, doctrines and practices of Freemasonry. This booklet is an essential tool in understanding the challenge of a pagan invasion that has infiltrated the core of Christianity itself.

Perfect Bound, 5x8, 40 Pages, $5.00
ISBN# 1-60039-181-8
TO ORDER, VISIT WWW.LAMPPOSTPUBS.COM

TO HELP YOU REVEAL THE TRUTH!

TO MORONI WITH LOVE
by ED DECKER

To Moroni With Love, is a loving, yet straightforward message to the millions of people who call themselves Latter-day Saints. It is a message of great importance from one former Mormon to those he left behind. Because of his deep love of Christ and his compassionate heart for those trying to serve God but mired in the "laws and ordinances" of a false gospel, Ed implores readers to take a look into the basic doctrines of Mormonism that separate it unconditionally from Christian orthodoxy.

Perfect Bound, 5x8, 44 Pages, $5.00
ISBN# 1-60039-179-6

TO ORDER, VISIT WWW.LAMPPOSTPUBS.COM

www.ingramcontent.com/pod-product-compliance
Lightning Source LLC
Chambersburg PA
CBHW052045070526
44584CB00018B/2612